The Song of Set

a poem by

Judith Page

ISBN-13: 978-1507768419

ISBN-10: 1507768419

Æon of Set painting by Judith Page

I dedicate this poem to the late Kenneth Grant,

Don Webb and the late

Billie Walker John, who in life was a Universal Setian

About the Author

©Joe Page

Judith Page was born in Australia. She graduated from Chelsea School of Art in London. She is a respected painter specializing in representations of Egyptian Pantheon groups with a strong emphasis on astronomy. Her work has featured on covers of numerous magazines and books. She is a great storyteller and poet, and brings the mystery and magic of Egypt alive.

OTHER BOOKS BY THE AUTHOR

Song of Bast

Song of Meri-Khem

Song of the Ibaru

Theft of the 7 Ankhs

Pathworking with the Egyptian Gods

Invocations to the Egyptian Gods

Angelic Magick

Realm of Angels

Contents

Acknowledgements

Foreword

Author's notes

I   Introduction

II   Day of Manifestation

III   Song of Nut

IV   Birth of Set

V   Khemit

VI   Solar Power

VII   The Two Brothers

VIII   Heb Sed Festival

IX   Heb Sed Two

X   Æon of Set

XI   The Meeting

Explanatory notes on Heb Sed Two Festival

Glossary

Contact the author

Further Information

Acknowledgements

For their valuable assistance of this work, I give grateful thanks to my cousin the late Sir Kenneth Trezise OBE, my partner Alain Leroy, Caroline Wise, Michael Staley, and Paul F Newman.

Foreword

Judith Page is what the great Omm Sety would have called: 'One of the *real* ones...' When she evokes the inner realms, be assured that she does so as a seasoned traveller within them.

In writing this poem Judith has attempted to cut through so much of what we now think of as Ancient Egypt, and only the bare bones will remain. Symbolic figureheads such as Osiris and Amon will be discussed, but not elevated, and favoured centres of apparent importance or popularity will be by-passed. This will not be a book for those who wish to play tourist, dropping off here for a quick sensation, or stopping there for an imagined photo-shoot, it will be an experience for all those who wish to embrace the origin and notion of Set, and Set's values. In recording the mythical life of Set, Judith has applauded him. The strength and warmth of his intellect demand similar warmth in his dramatic performance throughout ancient Egyptian history. To adopt an attitude of detachment, particularly towards the ancient and unknown, can bar from sight those many scenes glimpsed by the historian who approaches the role of reconstructing an era with sympathy, insight and understanding. Neither the truth nor the equilibrium of scholarship is disturbed by controlled imagination and honest praise of this much-maligned Egyptian god. She is portraying the mythological concept and personality of Set not in order to worship a hero, but to recognise him as a leader and a hero. Set strives to take his stand against 5,000 years of a 'drift of history' with the introduction of Osireion and Amonite tradition, and a preconditioning before being replaced by Christianity.

Alan Richardson author of *Inner Guide to Egypt*

Author's notes

I write this poem for my dear friend, the late Billie Walker-John. She was an extraordinary person, whose passing in the year 2000 affected me deeply. Although originally from America, she spent the last part of her life in Gwent, South Wales, with her husband Nigel and ten cats. Towards the end of her life she never ventured beyond the shores of Britain. When she stayed with me in London she would tell me how her spirit continuously ventured to the ancient realms of Egypt.

In 1990 Billie co-wrote *Inner Guide to Egypt* with Alan Richardson. The book was, for her, the culmination of thirty years of fascination with, and devotion to, Pharaonic Egypt. It also marked the end of her magickal apprenticeship.

Owing to the limitations she had to conform to regarding the above publication, a great deal of the work she had envisaged was left out. In order to finish off the work she started in her own short lifetime, in a sense I write this with her and, through her. The plan and the outline are both from her, as she visits seven specific centres in ancient Egypt in order to touch upon the essence of that most slandered, feared and criticized of all the gods, Set, Prince of Darkness. This is not just a journey that she always wanted to do in life, but also a piece of magick that can now be achieved after her death.

This poem is also written for and about Set, as a stand against such dogmatic philosophies of religious history. Protest is needed: since the middle to late kingdom this emphasis of Set and his influence has passed from histiography into our culture at large. So much of our current literature and thought rejects the role of the scapegoat in mythology, denies the importance of his individual genius in social change, refuses to recognise his superiority, and has a fear of uniqueness and discord.

The fatalistic approach that informed authoritarians have taken regarding the Set figure, has received increasingly influential support, while the various concepts of him have appeared in varied guises. It is quite apt to quote A L Kroeber's 'deep-seated, blind and intricate forces that shape culture'. The hero is a particle caught in the drift of religious and cosmic history, a mere by product and what happened, had to happen.

In this Ur-Egypt, it is the Pantheon group of Osiris, Re and all the other 'good' Gods of Egypt who are the usurpers, the intruders. It is the sovereignty of Set they seek to overthrow, not the other way around; an eldritch worship they must overturn and vanquish. This they do to become the victors, the 'Good Guys' of a sun-lit Egypt filled with their worship. The stellar darkness of the oldest Egypt is overturned, demonised and rejected but not forgotten. The worship of Set, his liturgies and images, seep through into the religions of the solar gods the old ways always remain in Egypt. In this regard, they act as the backdrop against which the victors develop.

It is my intent in this book to return the backdrop to its original primacy, to reveal what came before the victors, to provide the inner guide to Set. We tend today, due to our Western Judeo-Christian conditioning, to see this older Set and his landscape as stereotyped 'evil' that is always destined to be overcome by the equally stereotyped 'good'. This conditioning usually tends to narrow its focus on the viewpoint of the 'good guys', the winners. Only rarely do we consider the viewpoint of the 'bad guys', the demonised or conquered. Maybe we do not want to hear what it will tell us about ourselves.

In this book we let Set figuratively speak for himself. We feel it is time to hear his side of the story. He has only had to wait 5,000 years for it to be told.

Set has become a controversial figure in recent historical researches and discussion, but all the facts are not being disclosed. Scholars have attempted to strip him of his reputation for originality and genius, harmony and pure brotherly love by maintaining that his chaotic actions universally were something to be highlighted and condemned. They have called attention to his murderous ways and continued alienation of all things harmonious.

Whoever delves into the fathomless secrets of the land of the Nile, or is held captive by the fascination of the five millennia of history before the Christian era, cannot help but admire the great kings of ancient Egypt who worshipped and fought under the name of Set and continued to bring both fame and fortune to this black land. Whatever the true judgement of Set's personality and forbearing as the first son of Nut, is discussed in this poem and will help to provide a more valid interpretation of his true nature.

I

Introduction

Should you ask me?

Why this story?

Why this tale of indoctrination?

Why of chaos and confusion?

Why the stand against religious dogma?

Within the dankness of the temples,

Against the backdrop of the desert,

And the limitless questing upwards,

Caught in the drift of cosmic history,

Plunged into depths of degradation,

Why has Sutekh been forsaken?

I should answer, I should tell you,

From the land of starry shadows,

From the sand-dunes and the desert,

Within the sanctuary of the temple,

The drama, the performance of a deity,

Help to shape in varied guises,

He of strength, warmth and bearing,

He of insight and understanding.

He the scapegoat of myth and history,

Was denied the importance of his genius.

Denied the cunning of his survival.

Through 5,000 years, drift of history

Set strives again to take his stand.

In the black land by the old Nile,

Against the Osirians and oppressors,

Against the Christian and the Muslim,

Against the scholar and history maker,

Who dared to strip him of his titles,

Of what happened, had to happen.

A mere particle, caught in a wrangle.

A shaper of worldly concepts,

Of notions uniquely ordered,

Set rises throughout triumphant.

We seek not to worship him,

But honour and applaud him.

We seek not to judge him,

But recognise and reward him.

We seek not to follow him,

But elevate and restore him.

II

Day of Manifestation

In the core of central stillness,

Lay the being, yet to come into being.

Knowing of itself by way of reasoning,

Mirrored thought-forms back and forth.

Myriads of atoms ever evolving,

Within them the primeval Logos,

Reflecting as the Great Eternal.

Out of this the climax of creating,

Along states of knowing, and consciousness,

Reaching a further stage of knowing.

Layer upon layer of folds in process,

Reaching a greater stage of knowing.

Layer upon layer, of folds in action,

Layer upon layer, forming anew.

Forming ever, aware of its knowing,

Supreme Logos in its being.

After a limitless time in motion,

Of great action and energising,

Came a time of greater stillness,

Came a Day of Manifestation.

An end created, out of which was born

A new phase of coming into being.

Came forth the grand order of matter.

From out of the One came all.

Complete in this order of being.

Complete in its coming into being.

Passive giving way to active.

From out of chaos, unity.

Came the great laws of creation.

Thus emerged the First One.

Taught the great whirling motion,

Taught the stirring of the eternal,

And the organism of the Infinite within.

III

Song of Nut

In the unremembered ages,

In the nights that are forgotten,

Downward through the starry cosmos,

From a far-ff constellation,

Fell the beautiful night enchantress

Born in mystery of heavenly star-dust,

Out of the water's celestial abyss,

In the moonlight, and the starlight,

Her form sparkling like a diamond.

Eyes of crystal shone like orbs,

Arched her body o'er the sky.

She sings a song of exaltation,

Intoning sounds of celestial spheres.

Of harmonious spinning patterns,

Ever changing designs of heaven,

The star body, paradise Mother,

Beloved Nut of the starry skies,

Blessed by Nu, Father to all gods,

Gave her Sothis as her kingdom.

Shining splendid was her prize.

Nut, enchantress of stellar heavens.

Nut, goddess of the seven stars.

IV

Birth of Set

In the moonlight and the starlight,

Between the dark night light'ning flashes,

Grips the infinite star-dust body,

Bursting outward from her bright side,

Came the firstborn of her children,

With her first voice she proclaimeth,

'He is My eldest, My beloved,

With whom I am well pleased'.

Born of darkness from the starlight,

Thus came the child of wonder.

Knew he the heavenly daughter.

Knew he the beauty of the stars,

Set loved his mother with carnal pleasure,

Feeding on the milk of space-dust.

Sut-Typhon, the first boy-child,

The first opener of the way,

Set the God, and Nut Goddess,

Ruled expanses of the heavens,

Ruled the blackened land of Khemit,

And the deserts and the wasteland,

Drifted he upon the west-wind,

Freedom, courage were his by-words.

Came a time he heard his destiny,

'Thou art doomed to wander far,

Thou wilt know the ancient wisdom,

But the ears of man will close.

Thou wilt know the wrath of many,

Feel the pain of your lost children.

By the east-wind, false and faithless,

Comes a tribal horde of murderers

To rewrite history for the masses.

So did Sutekh hear the tidings,

Listen did he to the old ones,

Little did he care for these words,

He the first-born of the Bright one,

Roamed the deserts and the wasteland,

Drifted he upon the west-wind,

Dreaming of his gentle mother.

V

Khemit

Out of Africa came the animals,

Came the totems of the shamans,

The ancient priests who shaped a nation,

Worked the magick of the scorpion,

Worked the lore of the seven stars,

Built the temples to the star-gods.

Out of reeds and poles they built them,

Placed the totems of the deities

In to the sanctuaries on the altars.

Worshipped Sutekh, Nut and Serquet.

Honoured Uazet and Meret-seger.

Cobra goddess, revered and powerful,

Gave her wisdom, spirit and charm.

Zones of power came to Khemit,

Sacred was the land of Sutekh.

Hapuy was the river Nile god.

Happy was the tribal nation.

Hunter-gatherer settled northward.

The brotherhood of man was form'd.

Thus the star-cult grew in numbers.

Thus established were the earth nomes,

Based on Siriun cosmic lore.

Hence their day began at sunset.

On the horizon of the west land,

Nut nightly gathered in the great sun,

Passing through her sacred body,

Spilling out the starry night.

The Dog-star and Ursa Major,

Washed down by the Milky Way.

Then the heavens were divided,

The land of Khemit split in two,

Set's dominion in the south land,

Manifesting the light of Nut,

She the ruler of the north land,

Giver of light out of darkness,

First time-keeper of the ancients.

Her body, supporter of the pillars,

Pillars that held the sky aloft,

Supporting all the heavenly bodies,

Where the Sun-god travelled daily,

Swallowed by her in the night.

Every night he was the aged god, Atum,

With his re-birth in the morning,

As the naked boy-child Horus.

Thus the ancients loved their goddess,

Loved her nightly in the dark skies.

Then the lunar replaced the stellar,

Days converged upon the night sky,

Twenty eight lunar houses founded,

Thirty-six nomes of ten assembled,

Created was the lunar calendar,

Mirrored on the land of Khemit,

From the starry heavens above her.

Came along a new time-keeper,

Lord Djehuti was his first name,

Bird-beaked dignitary roamed the skies.

But fugitive were the lunar timings,

Unstable were the lunar days,

Cast out were the lunar children,

Thus the dark god faced the light,

Phased in was the solar day.

VI

Solar Power

From the desert sands of Abdjw,

To the lush and green Men Nefer,

Upwards to Khenemu city,

The solar worship came to Khemit.

They built the temples and the pyramids,

Built them high in Re's reflection.

Glorified the name of Horus.

Gave his name to all the Pharaohs,

But Set's name was not forgotten.

There reigned many in his shadow:

Dual kingdoms thus existed,

Double capitals in the black land,

Nekhbet in the upper region,

Protected by the vulture goddess,

Wajdet in the lower kingdom,

Watched over by the serpent one.

Double crowns were thus created,

Crowns of Upper and Lower Egypt.

Red and white were the colours,

Colours of the double children,

Set and Horus sons of Nu'it,

Both adorning Pharaoh's forehead,

Wears the Sekhemti that held the power,

Uniting two lands, south and north.

Double headed was Sut-Horus,

Dual in nature was their purpose,

Night and Day were these two brothers,

Sut who opens, Heru closes.

Then came to passing the injustice.

Thus to Sutekh was given darkness,

Horus gains the light of day.

He becomes the supreme opener,

The Light, the ever-coming Sun,

Sut-Har of the Two Horizons,

Har-Iu, the ever-coming son.

Usurpers take o'er the land of Khemit,

Down from Asia they did wander.

Seized the land without authority,

Brought their gods of death and stasis,

Took the ancient realms of old ones.

Andjeti lost his throne to Enki,

Enki changed his name to Asar,

Stole from him his fine regalia,

His plum'ed head-dress of ostrich feather,

His crook and flail of ancient shepherds,

Garbed in wrappings like Udimu,

Spreading the new word of salvation.

But he needed a new consort,

To fill the gap of this staged mystery.

Hence was found the Libyan Isa,

Goddess of the Western province.

Not content with this new persona,

Rewrote the myth of ancient Nu'it,

Of the great unmated mother.

Then created gods Shu and Tefnut,

Twin lions of east and west land,

Who gave birth to Geb and Nu'it,

Brother and sister in the cosmos,

Whose children were five in number,

Asar and Heru, Set and Isa,

Nephthi was the last to follow.

Five extra days were gained in number,

Added to the lunar calendar.

From the temple voices rang out,

'The Lord of all has entered this world'.

Asar, saviour of this Khemit nation,

Took to wife his sister Isa,

Nephthi follows by marriage to Sutekh.

Thus was created a final grouping,

That would imprint for generations.

VII

The Two Brothers

Further insult adds to injury,

Set is upstaged by this brother.

Reigning king on earth was Asar,

Saving mankind from the old gods,

Giving laws and standards many,

Teaching farming in this scorched land,

Brewing beer from the harvest barley.

So this man was hailed and worshipped,

Made a deity over all gods.

The many nations grew and prospered,

Under the ægis of this man-wonder.

Then a plot was hatched by Sutekh,

To rid the black land of this poser.

Taking measure of Asar's body,

He then fashions a splendid coffer,

Rich in woods and polished metal,

Holds a party in Asar's honour.

After drinking and merrymaking,

Presents the coffer for all to lie in.

Tempts the many with this great prize,

But it only fits this brother,

Laying down in his coffer neatly,

Sutekh slams the lid down on him,

Nails and solders down the fasteners.

On the seventeenth day of Athyr,

When Ra was in the sign of Scorpius,

Flings this coffer in the great Nile.

It came to pass the coffer floated

With the body of Asar inside.

To the far-off land of Byblus,

Where it settled on this seashore.

Around the coffer a great tree grew,

Folding Asar in its centre.

The king of Byblus saw this fine tree,

Cut it down for his grand palace.

There it joined the many pillars

In the courtyard for all to marvel.

Isa journeyed to this far land,

Found her brother's wooden coffer,

Within the pillar of the courtyard.

She wailed and wept her tears of sorrow,

Lamented for her long dead brother.

Sat she down by the town well,

Disguis'ed as a simple woman.

Then came passing the queen's maidens,

Stayed and chatted with the stranger.

Isa groomed and braided their hair,

Perfumed their fair skin with fine oils.

When the queen of Byblos smelt them,

Called upon this stranger woman,

Gave her comforts of the palace,

Gave her sole charge of her baby.

But the child fell in a fever,

Death came knocking on the child's crib

Isa fearful for her small charge,

Used her power and her magick,

Drove out the demons that so threatened,

Saved the small child from its sure death,

Returned the queen's child to its mother.

Joy and laughter filled the palace,

Gladdened were the royal parents,

Thus bestowed a gift to Isa,

Of gold and gemstones in abundance.

But Isa settled not for these gifts,

'Give me that great wooden pillar'

All exclaimed 'Why this pillar'

'It contains my loved one's body'.

'Take it with you my good woman'

Spake the great just king of Byblus.

Isa claimed the wooden coffer,

In a boat she sailed for Khemit,

With the body of her dead love,

Thus returned the fateful couple.

Remained in hiding was this goddess,

Lest the omens turn against her.

Far-off murmurs reached Set, her sibling,

Ever-seeking this other brother,

Found him hidden in the desert,

Cut him up in fourteen pieces,

Scattering them to far-off places.

Those that fell on Khemit's black land,

Formed the zones for hallowed worship.

But his phallus fell not earthward,

Went it to the watery Nile god,

Eaten by a silvery scaled fish,

Lodged forever in this being.

Helped by her sister Nephthi,

Gathered far flung limbs together,

Bound and wrapped them in pure linen.

Laid them on a stony altar,

Praying that he would recover.

Now gone was Asar's manhood,

Causing Isa to weep anew.

Worked her magick deep in mystery,

Then as a kite she hovered o'er him,

And with a phallus made of metal,

The precious metal gold of Ombos,

From Sutekh's realm in the southland.

Such was this strange unearthly union,

Of kite and dead god joined together,

Giving her the longed-for baby,

Horus, sun child, king of all.

Once more was Sutekh's patience tested,

Not contented with this last feat,

Hunted high and low for Horus.

Why should he once again be cheated?

By these usurpers, these newcomers?

Why had his mother Nui't left him?

Had he not been the perfect first-born?

But this hindered not Man's ambition,

Craving that which is immortal,

To be like gods, the everlasting.

But in life's long quest for the eternal,

They lost sight of all true meaning.

Hoodwinked were they by these notions,

Fed by the priesthood of Osiris.

Saviour, Christ-like in his suff'rings,

Died on earth and rose again.

Sent to this world to lead us all.

Convenient was the pharaoh's wisdom,

To banish Sutekh from his kingdom,

When times were good and many prospered.

But when the warlike tribe lands threatened,

They then rolled out Sutekh's statues,

Placed was Set above Osiris,

Oils and incense burned in censers,

In the temples and the courtyards,

High flew the banners in his honour,

Red, gold and black were his colours.

The god's black semen was daily gathered,

From the sand-dunes and the deserts,

These iron globules that fell earthward,

From the heavens of the cosmos.

Gathered were they in abundance,

To forge the sacred adze of Sutekh,

An ancient object made in the pattern

Of the great bear in the heavens,

Ursa Major of the seven stars.

VIII

Heb Sed Festival

During the sacred month of Khoiak,

When the river Nile subsided,

The Heb Sed festival returneth,

To honour the jubilee of Pharaoh.

Renewal was this ancient practice,

Of the king to all his people,

Mediator between earth and heaven,

Attended by the princely kin.

Lords and Ladies of the black land,

Scribes and priesthoods of the temples,

Paid homage to the shrines and deities,

Burnt incense to them for their favour,

Invoking their attention on him,

To give him strength and mighty courage.

Many days walked he in procession,

With the statues and their priesthoods,

Carried the royal placenta bundle.

Fan-bearers and the royal attendees

Made solemn pledges to the Pharaoh,

Seated then upon his gold throne.

His feet were washed in ancient practice,

Continued he to the robing room,

Donned the vestments for the ceremony,

Proceeded to a double throne.

Double was the Khemit kingdom,

Double was the Heb Sed ritual,

Twinning was the king's pavilion,

On the courtyard of Sakkara.

Alternate sittings on the two thrones,

Asserting power o'er the black land.

Then he crosses the temple courtyard,

Carried then upon a litter,

Preceded by the falcon standard,

To the sacred Horus chapel,

Receives the flail, crook and sceptre,

Wrapped in a cloak and four times proclaim'd,

Receiving homage from his loyal subjects,

With many blessings from the old ones,

Making generous off'rings to them,

He then removes his cloak of white wool.

Clad only in a kilt of linen,

And a tail of animal kind,

Dons the crown of Upper Egypt,

Carries a whisk and golden sceptre.

Four times running around the courtyard,

Returning to the jackal deity,

Offers up his royal insignia,

And carried again upon a litter,

To the sacred Sutekh chapel,

Receives the flail, crook and sceptre,

Cloaked in red and four times proclaim'd,

Repeats the marathon o'er again.

Concludes the testing feats of vigour,

Pharaoh re-visits the sacred chapels,

Horus of Edfu and Set in Ombos.

Raised his mighty bow of ash-tree,

Seized his arrows, jasper-headed,

Where he shoots these victory arrows,

To the major cardinal points.

A re-enactment of his enthronement,

A test and trial of true king ship,

Where Set and Horus judged him justly.

Ancient was this celebration,

A Heb Sed season of renewal.

IX

Heb Sed Two

Let us take this one step further,

To another kind of temple,

A Solar structure built by Khufu,

To celebrate his life re-newal,

Not a grave to hold his body.

Not a place of lasting doom,

Pharaoh knew the secret wisdom.

Knew he the ways of Sutekh;

He did honour this ancient deity,

Pledged to keep the hallowed way.

On this sacred mound called Rostau

Where the pyramids stand gleaming,

Clad in the finest, whitest limestone,

Gold-capped in Aurichalcum,

Brilliant in Egypt's sunshine,

From the Rostau valley gather

The many priesthoods and their deities,

As they wind their snakelike walking,

To this temple on the skyline.

Many drums beat out a rhythm,

Fanfares of trumpets hail the entrance,

Preparing for the king's arrival.

The air is stilled at this moment,

When Pharaoh takes his first step forward,

Ra's last rays shine on this man-god.

Dress'd in his fine regalia,

He wears the double crown of Khemit,

White and Red of Heru- Sutekh.

Across his broad chest hangs a collar,

Inlaid with many precious gemstones,

Each one perfect in its setting,

Around his waist he wears a gold sash,

Hanging from this his long white tunic;

Crisply pleated in pure spun linen,

Golden are his woven sandals,

Softly touching the scorching dry sand.

In his right hand he firmly carries,

Crook, flail and Uwas sceptre.

Surrounded by the many faces,

Regarding Pharaoh with jubilation.

But Pharaoh is not with those present,

He is elsewhere in this drama,

He alone will share the secrets,

He alone will run the gamut,

All alone to prove he's mighty.

The hands of priest are now upon him,

Taking from him crown and vestments.

Clad only in his white tunic,

Walks final steps in meditation.

Facing him the portal beckons,

Darkened is the passage onward.

Upright walks he in the dim light,

To a narrow wooden ladder.

Up he climbs, then stoops now forward,

His body bending over double,

Crawling slowly like a wolf-dog,

Upward goes he seeing nothing,

Two and seventy steps he scrambles,

When at last he is now upright,

Lifts his gaze up to the cavern.

A corbelled ceiling gallery welcomes,

Strange sounds filter downward to him,

Causing him to swoon with pleasure.

Two steep stairways cling to side walls,

Centred by a deeper hallway.

Much perplexed is this proud Pharaoh,

Which way should he choose to go,

Masked and cloaked in a fine skin,

The Sem priest ushers this king upwards,

By the left hand stair he travels.

Three and ninety are these steep steps,

Counting as he climbs and ponders.

A wooden ladder leading upward,

Seven rungs are on this ladder,

Pausing now above the gallery,

To catch his breath he pushes onward.

Stooping once again he walks on,

Standing tall for a brief moment,

To stoop a while before he enters,

In to the huge and inner sanctum.

Of Sutekh, child of Nu'it.

In this great room stands assembled

A priesthood pois'ed, and alerted,

To test this king-god to his limits.

Chamber walls of black lined granite,

Ring with vowel sounds from the many,

In this great room's floor is centred

The large red coffer, empty, ready.

He seems to float as chanting rises,

Lowered is he into this stone bed.

Positioned is his fragile body,

His head is laid down to the south end,

Feet in the direction northward;

In this chasm he lays suspended,

While the Sem priest utters soul sounds,

Four Wahab priests stand at the corners;

Hands placed on the sacred coffer,

Making vowel sounds for the rebirth,

Sounds that penetrate his being.

No more does he see the priesthood,

Altered states of mind he's sensing.

The coffer now begins to vibrate,

With mingled sounds of much intoning.

Pharaoh's body is in suspension,

No more do his veins hold red blood;

The king is filled with such vibration,

As he's raised to cosmic levels,

Much mystery is now told to him,

Listens to this multi-format,

To a different time continuum.

But this is only preparation,

This is not the final setting,

Raised now up he stands erected,

Sem priest stepping forward to him,

Leaving Sutekh's sacred chamber,

Returning to the corbelled gallery

In the manner he was directed,

Backwards he walks down the stairway

To the narrow hall'd entrance,

For the next phase of his journey,

To the reverse side of his soul.

Backwards he walks now doubled,

Through the tunnel to the chamber.

Hallowed is this space to Heru,

Grey-lined are the walls of this room,

In this great room's floor is centred,

White and gleaming is the coffer,

Pure limestone this is hewn from,

Ringing out are strange tonations.

Once again his body's lowered,

Downward to a different level,

No more does he sense the priesthood,

Removed are they from his vision.

Backwards through the void he plummets,

Deeper still his body's falling,

Through the inner space of no-thing.

Then crossing o'er this greater abyss,

Feels the might of serpent current,

Within this realm are Sutekh's tunnels,

Mirrored backward to times primeval,

Into the void of formless conscience,

Plummets down into the abyss.

Sensing now a fearsome crushing,

Thus awakening the conscience in him,

Where all polarity loses meaning.

Now much exalted by this magick,

Appears to Pharaoh in this dream state,

Thus awakens the ancient fire snake

Envelops the crown part of his forehead,

Awakening power zones from non-being.

Around him scarlet dust is swirling,

Out of a black sun never setting,

In radiant light appeareth Sutekh,

Pure embodiment of the first-one,

Revealing secrets to this Pharaoh.

Knowing is he of this wisdom,

He hath met the child of Nui't.

Spake He to him words of power,

XEPER-A XEPER XEPER-U

I am He who came into being,

And in coming into being,

Created the being's who came into being,

Came he out of the great un-being,

Unmanifested in the first time,

Who created all beings in Sutekh's image.

Thus Pharaoh returneth as he entered,

Moving his body in the adze shape,

Downward through the Sutekh tunnel,

Leaves the pyramid of Khufu,

Pharaoh returns complete, and altered,

Not as the mortal king of Egypt,

But as the future Set of old.

X

Æon of Set

From the great walls of the temples,

They took the chisels to the stonework.

No longer viewed was Sutekh's god name.

Then, covered were the many altars,

By a new more favoured image,

Brought was he from far off Judea,

Dwelt he in the hidden places,

Till a time when all were ready,

To proclaim him Christ the Lord.

But Sutekh walked within the shadows,

Kept his vigil on this new king,

Hence the Christ-folk called him Satan,

Blamed him for this Christ-being's suff'rings;

Was the cause of all temptation,

Maker of all things evil,

Sends the sickness and the pestilence,

Sends disease and death among us,

Sends the dark mist from the marshes,

Have we heard this song before?

So the white flame burned in heaven,

In the name of Heaven's god-child,

Bringing followers from all nations,

Spreading many tales of wonder,

Miracle stories reaching far lands.

But the priesthood knew a good thing,

They could once more gain control,

Hide all the sacred words of mystery,

In the halls they called the churches,

Separate the poorer classes,

From the rich and powerful gentry,

Behind the rood screens carved in cedar.

Took the freedom from the people.

Locked up every trouble-maker.

Hoodwinked once again by cunning,

Christ's law grew by many numbers,

In his name was fought the battles,

Crusaders marched and killed the pagans,

By this suff'ring they were blinded,

To the real truth of their history,

Felt forsaken by this new god.

So again they turned to Sutekh.

They did worship him in secret,

In the caverns well protected,

Return'ed to their ancient creedings,

Remade all their ancient vessels,

Sculptured once again his image,

Put him in a place of glory,

Burned the incense on their altars,

Wore the colours in his honour,

Reversed the holy Christian symbols.

Adorned their neck and hands bright ore,

Fashioned the inverted pentacle.

Shaitan took on many guises.

In this multi-form he flourished.

Gathered he his long lost children,

Re-taught them powers long forgotten.

Onward through the five millennia

Setians group together world-wide.

Sharing knowledge so long hidden,

Breaking down the evil barriers,

Unlocking all the secret libraries,

Cascading the much sought logos.

Came a force of great empow'ment,

Writers, artists and magick-makers,

Leaders in the field of culture.

In the name of Set they came forth,

Open faced and open handed,

Speaking truth to all who ask'ed,

Directing all to Shaitan's temple,

The Great Temple in our psyche.

Now unlocked, no longer guarded,

Lodged in true and open spirit.

Again We are great in numbers

As We walk along the left path,

Seeing now the evil-makers,

Who for centuries they killed us

In the name of one we honour.

Set's name rings across the cosmos,

Open are the future channels,

Free now is the Setian mind.

XI

The Meeting

Relax and slowly close your eyelids,

Take yourself back to far-off ages,

To Abdjw, city of the Neters,

Built by pharaohs in a desert.

Create a temple to the old gods,

Of palest sandstone rich in carving,

A temple structure steeped in mystery,

Inviting pilgrims to venture inside.

As you awaken to this dream state,

And taking your first step forward,

Climbing onward up a steep ramp,

Appears the temple in full view.

The sun is setting behind this god-house,

Ra's last rays dip gently westward,

Bathing the temple in a rosy glow.

Grit hangs heavy in your dry throat,

As desert sands give final gusts.

As you cross the temple courtyard,

Vision blurred by ancient phantoms,

Await you, the Wahab priests of Set.

Hairless are their well-oiled bodies,

Shaven are their gleaming heads,

Smelling of the sacred fragrance

Peculiar to the lord Sutekh.

The priests are naked to the waistline,

Linen bands swathed o'er their chest,

Hanging are their crisp white tunics.

To their ankles hangs the garment,

Of linen finely spun of thread.

They instruct you, 'take off your clothing,

These trappings of the outer world'

Then they wash you from the waters

Gushing from the Setereion.

Oiled with fragrance, and dressed in linen,

Making solemn promises before leaving,

Before you enter the hallowed sanctum,

Prepared are you to venture on.

Via the courtyard, you enter the temple.

Forests of pillars tower above you.

No walls are visible, only the pillars.

A darkness enters your core of being,

Ever cautious is your treading,

As the cool floor greets your hot feet.

Lonely walking in the darkness,

Thinking of what fate awaits you,

Conscious are you of the unseen,

Of watchers hidden in the shadows.

Walking upward a further level,

Your senses rising as you go,

Incense is wafted in your direction,

You follow the fragrant aroma deeper,

Into the closed house of the Neters,

Thinking of your sacred vows.

Then the shaking of a sistrum,

Pulls you sharply to your senses,

Makes you still your shaking body,

Before you then continue onwards,

Passing by the seven chapels,

That lead directly to the sanctuaries.

But once again you're halted

By a different music sounding,

Tones strangely unfamiliar to you,

That captures your attention.

Then, out of the darkness slowly,

Hidden deep among the shadows,

A Sem priest processes forward.

He, also, is completely shaven,

Like the Wahab priests of Sutekh,

His well-oiled golden body glistens;

In the faint light from the sconces,

He is robed in full regalia,

According to his rank and station.

His crisp white linen tunic rustles,

Gathered pleats around his waistline,

Held in place by Aurichalcum,

A golden belt of red and yellow,

Clasped by a golden-headed leopard,

Finely sculptured in great detail,

Hanging over his broad shoulders,

He wears the fur-skin of a leopard,

Worn only by the Sem priest,

Which echoes the great starry body,

Of the ever knowing Goddess,

Nu'it, of the seven stars.

Grasped firmly in his right hand,

He carries the gold Ur-hekau,

He speaks words of ancient wisdom,

That echo memories long forgotten,

These are strangely familiar to you.

As you gaze into his dark eyes,

Which pierce you as he searches deeply,

Why you choose to venture further,

Into the great house of the Neter.

Thus, please'd with his findings,

He leads you on through darkened chapels,

Pausing briefly outside each one,

Uttering sacred words of power,

Words solely for the Neters.

You then both continue onwards,

To the second inner sanctum,

Where he enters this room darkly,

And beckons you to follow swiftly.

Lifting up an ancient flagstone,

From the floor of this inner sanctum,

Reveals a tiny hidden stairway,

Leading down into the darkness.

He leaves you standing in this sanctuary,

To make your own way downwards,

Into the subterranean temple,

Built by Setians long before you,

To conceal the mysteries and the secrets,

From the faithless and the godless,

For a time which is now upon us.

So cautiously you climb downwards,

In the velvet black you wander.

Along a corridor never-ending,

You are confronted by the wolf-god,

Wepwawet in all his splendour.

He greets you, and beckons you to follow,

Further downward you both venture,

Your heart is racing in this silence.

Then a doorway concealed in sandstone

Flies open at the god's touch.

He then utters a sacred password,

You enter through the secret portal,

To a different kind of darkness.

You're standing in a room of grandeur,

Granite red walls hung with banners,

Red gold hangings ballooning gently,

By an inner wind within them.

The air is heavy with sweet aromas,

Like water drenching sun- hot sandstone,

Fresh cut hay in the grasslands,

Sandstorms of the annual Kham-sin

Sodden wood after much rain….

The floor of pure black quartz crystal,

Reflects a dimly lighted image.

Your attention shifts, as you gaze upwards.

The great god Set is before you

Ever wakeful, ever watchful,

In this sanctum, dimly lighted,

He sits upon a regal high throne,

Made of pure gold from Ombos,

He supports the Hedjet and the Deshert,

Crowns of Upper and Lower Egypt.

On his regal head He wears them.

His face is chiselled with fine emotion.

A gold collar hangs o'er His broad chest,

Black, gold and red is His tunic,

That gently defuses by the black flames,

Licking the edge of His high podium.

Holds the Uwas sceptre in His left hand,

Sculptured in His very likeness.

His amber eyes shine forth upon you

In the glimmering, flickering firelight,

As he bestows His gift of sight upon you

As you prepare, to come into your being.

Then there follows a great silence,

Even the very flames are quietened.

Out of this stillness Set breaks the silence,

With a voice of winds a'roaring,

Each distinct in its own message,

Notes resound across the quartz floor.

Words engulf you and fill your spirit,

With magick to be with you always,

He bestows His gift of sound upon you,

As you prepare to come into your being.

Stepping down lightly from His platform,

Walking through the flickering black flames,

Across the mirror polished quartz floor,

Set stands erect and tall before you.

His breath is on your mortal visage,

A breath likened to the sweet oil,

The priests so lavished on your body,

In preparation for this moment.

He bestows His gift of smell upon you,

As you prepare to come into your being.

Reaching out He touches your heart,

You are gripped by such emotion,

By His hand upon your body.

Dissolving right way through you.

He bestows His gift of touch upon you,

As you prepare to come into your being.

The very nearness of Him to you,

And the solitary five millennia,

Endured by Him in this sad world,

Makes you to shed tears of sorrow,

Tears that can easily fill an ocean.

From the shadows comes the weeping,

You hear the sobbing and lamenting,

He has cried for His lost children,

Now returned and finally gathered.

These tears He confers upon you,

As you prepare to come into your being.

You are made whole by His presence,

You *have* now come into your being.

Unable to speak to Set directly,

He fuses His very thoughts with yours.

He reveals the æons of His knowledge,

He speaks of the ancient past and present,

He tells you of the times to come.

In a state of deep, and dreamless sleeping,

In a state where mind is not,

In this sense, is empty of all thought,

Linking with the Universal Logos,

Dreaming of back dream sliding,

Of parallel world-beings,

Pooling of greater world thoughts,

Re-bonding of ancient receptors,

Merging with pure consciousness,

Feelings beyond elation, magnified.

All this, He gives unto you.

Your sixth sense is restored to you,

His gift of Xeper He bestows on you.

Silence follows this precious moment,

As you reflect on inner changes,

Set has put you through the trial,

You have found Him great and noble,

Just and fair and true of spirit.

Standing taller, stronger, knowing,

By His grace you make your exit,

Passing through the secret doorway,

Once more greeted by the wolf-god,

Escorts you to the temple proper.

But you see the ghosts no longer,

Hear no more the whispering spirits,

But the assembling of the priesthood.

The entire company, the Setian Temple

Robed in splendour, jewelled and perfumed.

Gathered are they in their great ranks,

Now regarding you with favour

Of your status, and your knowing

That you have come into you're being,

Now at one with your own kind.

See the many Setian faces,

Of the past, present, and future.

All walking on the left path,

As they come into their being.

Moonbeams cast their eerie lighting,

Down the many priest-holes falling,

Forming silvery pathways hither,

Light up worn and furrowed flagstones,

Across the broad expanse of temple.

Leaving halls and outer courtyards,

Leaving this great Setian temple,

Deep in knowledge of the Æon,

That Set empowers all who follow.

Now the darkness fills the night sky,

The stars of Nut come out to greet you,

As you take your place, in Sutekh's world.

--o00o--

Set the Return painting by Judith Page

Explanatory notes on the Heb Sed Two Festival

For centuries, since the Great Pyramid's chambers have been opened to the many visitors throughout the ages, archaeologists and Egyptologists have confused everyone with false notions of some fantastic burial place for the long deceased King Khufu.

Since no evidence has been discovered to support this idea of a final resting place for the king, I put it to you, that the so-called King and Queen's Chambers were used for another, and more significant purpose, other than burial.

We must first look at the Heb Sed Festival of renewal, and re-birth of the Pharaoh. This highly charged event would take place every 30 years of the king's reign, but in some of the earlier dynasties, it was celebrated more frequently.

An open space, such as the grand arena in front of Zoser's pyramid at Sakkara was prepared in respect for the two mighty deities, Set and Horus. This was known as the Heb Sed Court, flanked on both sides with the chapels of the Upper and Lower Egyptian gods of each nome.

The king would run in the open space between the two

rows of shrines dressed alternatively in the insignia colours of white for Upper, and red for Lower Egypt. This ritual race around the 'field' was repeated four times as the ruler of the South, and four times as ruler of the North.

This was indeed a very public occasion, witnessed by Pharaoh's subjects who not only regarded this as a great spectacle, but also put great store in the safe delivery of their king as he ran the 'gamut'.

But the true test of Pharaoh's strength was not to be physical. This test was indeed an act of rebirth and renewal of mind and spirit, and the ritual setting would have been the great pyramid of Khufu.

The king would be prepared in the usual manner i.e. in his stately regalia, and together with a retinue of priests and attendees, he would make his way from the valley of the Sphinx, up the flag stoned causeway, to the entrance of the Great Pyramid.

Pharaoh would then be relieved of his cape, sceptres and crowns, and remained dressed only in a short white linen kilt. After priestly blessings, he would then venture alone, through the pyramid entrance bearing the hieroglyph letter of the god Hapuy, and into the dimly lit corridor.

If we look at a cross section of the Great Pyramid of Khufu, we will notice that the passageways and shafts leading to the two chambers resemble the constellation of Ursa Major. We must also look at the corresponding link between the shape of the adze, fashioned out of the painstaking gathering of tektites from the surrounding desert, which were later smelted down to make this instrument.

As Pharaoh made his way up through the pyramid, he would then be reduced to the very form of the constellation of The Plough, which is also representative of the god Set. In this doubling, crawling and walking phase, the king proceeds to the so-called King's Chamber by way of the left-hand stairs up through the corbelled gallery.

For argument sake, I will call this room the Chamber of Set. There is nothing inside this great space, but for a large sarcophagus of red granite, the

orientation from the longest sides, south to north. The walls and floor are of black granite.

Priests would be present to aid Pharaoh as he was placed in the sarcophagus, head to the south and feet to the north, which signifies the position of the pole star in the north.

After the chanting of prayers the Sem priest would then signal the commencement of the ritualistic ordeal Pharaoh would be put through. Four priests would position themselves at either corner of the sarcophagus, and placing their fingertips on the edge of the coffer, would intone specifics vowel sounds. According to John Reid, a specialist in the study of Sonics, 'When certain sounds are played in close proximity to granite, these sound frequencies excite the crystals within the stone, which makes them resonate'.

Given that the entire chamber and sarcophagus is of granite, this would have brought about a physical, mental and spiritual change within the body and mind of the king. His very being would be saturated with sound. His limbs and vessels would be tingling due to the vibrations of this deliberate orchestration of tones, each priest emitting a prescriptive dose.

At a particular point, the Sem priest would indicate to the Wahab's, to gently remove Pharaoh from the coffer, and in a backwards or reversed mode, the king would leave the Chamber of Set. He would be fully prepared for his next phase of rebirth and renewal, which would take place in the room below, which I will call, the Chamber of Horus.

Walking backwards down the right hand side of the corbelled gallery, reversing along a corridor between the double stairway, bending double and still in reverse, Pharaoh would enter this next chamber. He would not see the priesthood, but would be aware of yet more chanting and intoning of carefully chosen notes which once again resonate through the granite. The walls of this chamber are lined with pale grey granite and in the centre of the floor is placed a gleaming white limestone sarcophagus of similar proportions to that of the coffer in the Chamber of Set.

Once again Pharaoh is guided and placed in the coffer. His emotions run high as he is plunged into the great abyss of the celestial waters. In trance, his body sleeps, but his soul is awake. It is active on its own plane; the body is in the background of a different matter. This mind-altering state has rid him of his fragile body, as he is absorbed into the realms of non-being. He is awakened to the super consciousness of that which IS, and everything that is portrayed, is of the events of the inner world by way of a mirroring. His conditions of focus are being determined by these emotional states.

He has been subjected to the very force of the Primum Mobile, and with this seventh ray of consciousness he has received Complete Initiation into the 'living death'. Thus, he has achieved the freedom of the spirit brought through to the plane of matter. He is free, empowered, and stands taller and greater amongst his fellow Man.

In those days, a Pharaoh was a man alone. He would have had the council of his Sem and the input of the Vizier etc., but after a Heb Sed festival of rebirth and renewal, this would make him supra human.

The very design of the Great Pyramid sets a platform for a magnificent and mind-altering stage for a special event. One can only enter this great monument today, to realise that there is something very special and poignant about the peculiar design quality of these tunnels and shafts, all hidden from public view. Who else but the ancient Egyptians would fashion a tunnel on the god Set's constellation of Ursa Major?

As we enter this great mound of calculated pieces of stone, our body's twist and double, we crawl and walk tall as did the pharaohs of old. We reach the inner sanctum, totally exhausted, and stand over an empty granite box where the king would have been plunged into his own kind of oblivion. We too are laid waste in this empty room, and some of us wonder what it's all about. Then, as we make our way down again to the outside world, we find that secretly and subliminally, the pyramid has given us back something else, in return for the energy we gave it, to breath new life into the Great Tunnels of Set.

Glossary

Abdjw : Ancient Egyptian name for Abydos

Abydos : Greek form of Abdjw

Abyss : The great gulf or void that constitutes separating individual consciousness from its universal source. To Cross the Abyss, or transcend the world of subject and object and resolve the antinomies of mundane consciousness.

Adze : Ancient ritual object made from iron tektites. It was fashioned in the shape of the constellation Ursa Major, The Great Bear or Plough. This also symbolised the god Set.

Andjeti : God in anthropomorphic form originally worshipped in the mid-Delta in the Lower Egyptian nome, 9.

Asar : Ancient Egyptian for Osiris. There are over

one hundred names of gods that start with the

prefix 'Asar'.

Athyr : Third month of the season of Akhet – winter –

inundation.

Atum : Sun-god and creator of the universe. The

name Atum, carries the idea of 'totality' in the sense

of an ultimate and unalterable state of perfection.

Aurichalcum : Mysterious red flecked gold, thought to

have originated from the mythical Atlantis.

Byblus : A Syrian port.

Chaos : The primal substance that is, paradoxically,

by no means substantial, out of which the illusion

of formless primordial Matter appears to rise.

Crook : Emblem of sovereignty and divinity.

Deshert : Red crown of Lower Egypt in the North.

Djehuti : (or Thoth in Greek) The Moon god and patron

of the sciences in ancient Egypt, who presides over

scribes and knowledge. He was worshipped in the First Dynasty.

Dog-star : (see Sirius)

Edfu : A city located in Upper Egypt called Behdet by the ancient Egyptians. Edfu was the capital of the second nome of Upper Egypt, and the cult centre of Horus the falcon god.

Enki : (or Ea) 'Lord of the Earth' – God of Mesopotamia.

Flail : Emblem of sovereignty and dignity.

Geb : Earth-god and president of the divine tribunal on the kingship according to the Osirian mythology.

Great Eternal : The unmanifest made pure existence.

Hapuy : God of the annual Nile inundation. The god is shown in human form with aquatic plants on his head.

Har-Iu : Means, the 'Coming Son' of a two-fold
nature.

Heb Sed : An elaborate ceremony of the king's
coronation, his 'Sed' festival or jubilee and ultimate
burial, were twice repeated with the different
insignia, architecture and customs of Upper and
Lower Egypt. The ceremony of the 'Running of
Apis' appears to have been closely associated with
the Sed Festival, but it seems more likely to have
been originally a celebration of the festival called
the 'Birth of the god Sed'. The entire nation was
deeply concerned with the celebration of these
important rites.

The festival usually took place thirty years
after the king's accession to the throne. However,
according to the evidence of the Palermo Stone, the
Sed festival was celebrated by some of the archaic

kings repeatedly, and at much shorter intervals

than the accepted thirty year period.

In order to celebrate this important festival, a

special building was erected, called a Sed Pavillion.

This included a Throne Room and a Robing Room

in which the king changed his garments and insignia

according to the various double rites connected

with the two lands.

But most important was the Heb-Sed Court, flanked

on both sides with the chapels of the Upper and

Lower Egyptian gods of each nome.

The king would run in the open space between the

two rows of shrines dressed alternatively in the

insignia colours of white for Upper, and red for

Lower Egypt. This ritual race around the 'field' was

repeated four times as the ruler of the South, and

four times as ruler of the North. It is suggested that

the 'field' represented Egypt and the ritual race

perhaps signified to all those present, his claim as

possessor of the land. To this was added the further

impetus for national fertility - his actions made the

land fruitful and productive.

Hedjet : White crown of Upper Egypt in the South.

Heliopolis : Greek form of Khemenu

Her-Sutekh : Twin form of Horus and Set.

Heru : Ancient Egyptian for Horus.

Horus : Greek form of Heru.

Isa : Ancient form of Isis.

Isis : Greek form of Isa.

Judea : A country on the Eastern Mediterranean

Kham-sin : Seasonal sandstorm in Lower Egypt.

The storm period was long viewed as a season of

contagious diseases and illnesses.

Khemit : A name applied to Egypt as the black or red

land. The black or red Nilotic mud that literally
formed Egypt.

Khemenu : Ancient Egyptian for Heliopolis.

Khemit : (see Khem)

Khoiak : Fourth month in the season of Akhet.

Khufu : Reigned between 2551 – 2528 – Old Kingdom.
He was the Pharaoh who built the Great Pyramid.

Kite : Isis took the form of this bird to copulate with
her brother Osiris.

Men Nefer : Ancient Egyptian form of Memphis.

Meret-seger : Cobra-goddess dwelling on the mountain
that overlooks the valley in western Thebes. Her
name means 'she who loves silence'.

Nekhbet : Vulture goddess of Nekheb upholding the
king's sway in Upper Egypt.

Nephthi : (or Nephthis in Greek) Fifth child of Nut and
Geb, according to the Osirian pantheon mythology.

Neter : Ancient Egyptian for a god.

Nomes : Pharaonic Egypt was divided into forty-two administrative districts, or nomes. Each nome had principal deities.

Nu : (or Nun) God personifying the primeval waters out of which emerged the creator-god. Nu is the 'father to all gods' but this emphasises only his unrivalled antiquity as an element of the Egyptian cosmos – in terms of importance, he is superseded by the creator sun-god Atum.

Nuit : 'Infinite Space and the Infinite Stars thereof'. In a metaphysical sense, Nuit is the Continuum of Paradise that results from the resolution of mundane being into the elements of non-being. Nuit is represented as a human female form arched over the earth as in the Stele of Revealing. In a more specialised and magickal sense, she is the compliment of Set. She is North, and compares

with Set, whose opposite is Horus in the South.

Nut : (see Nuit)

Ombos : The Set-worshipping tribes occupying a large

area in Upper Egypt called Ombos. This area was

also famous for the mining of gold.

Osirian : A follower of Osiris.

Osiris : Greek form of Asar.

Pharaoh : Derived from Har-Iu, which means the

Coming Son of a two-fold nature, and of the two IU

Houses.

Ra : (see Re)

Rannut : Ancient form of the cobra-goddess.

Re : Creator sun-god of Khenemu (or Heliopolis).

Rostau : Necropolis containing the pyramid fields was

known as the Duat or Rostau. A gateway, or

entrance.

Royal placenta bundle : The king's placenta called the 'Sacred Bundle of Life' is taken and preserved at the time of his birth. It is kept wrapped in the form of a kidney shape, for the entirety of the king's life. Ceremonially carried on a high pole by the Sem priest at all festive occasions it is buried with the king at the point of his death. (see Sem priest)

Sakkara : A plateau overlooking the ancient city of Men Nefer. Its vast courtyard or 'field' was used for the celebration of the Heb-Sed festival.

Satan : The Opposer; the Adverse and Averse One, and therefore the reflection or double that is the Devil, in the sense of existing as the opposite of Being.

Scorpius : Star constellation of Scorpio, and symbol of Serqet the scorpion goddess.

Sekhemti : The Red and White crowns of Upper and

Lower Egypt produced the Double Crown,

a combination of the two emblems.

Sem priest : the chief or High Priest. He also held the

first and most honourable station as the one who

offered sacrifice and libation in the temple - the

highest post - He appears to have been

called 'the prophet' and his title in the hieroglyphic

legends is 'Sem'. The Sem priest was the only

person who was lawfully allowed to kill the king

if he proved unable to continue to rule the land of

Khem. This would be as a result of not being able

to meet the test of the Heb-Sed, becoming gravely

ill being or perhaps mortally wounded in

battle. One of the most famous of Sem priest was

Setne Kha'muaset, favourite and most royal son of

Rameses II. Apart from having the responsibility

for arranging the many Heb-Sed festivals for his

father the king, this particular priest was probably

the first Egyptologist of those times to actually set

about restoring the Sakkara plateau. This would

have included the many pyramids and temples,

some of which were already two thousand years old.

Serqet : The scorpion –headed goddess whose name

became identified with the circle. Her stellar symbol

is Scorpio, which is the meaning of her name. The

Circle – to which she also gave her name – was

identified by the ancient Egyptians with the cyclic

revolutions of the star sacred to the god Set,

i.e. Sothis.

Set : (or Sut) The primordial god of the ancient

Egyptians; no earlier god exists in the recorded

history of the present human race. The word 'soot' is

derived from this incalculably ancient name. Set is

also the prototype of Shaitan or Satan, God of the

South whose star is Sothis. Set, or Sut (literally
meaning 'black') is the chief colour (or kala) of Set.
Black indicates the dark mysteries of this god which
were originally enacted in the underworld, 'nether'
world, or Amenta. The god is Lord of Amenta, or
'hidden land' - in other words, Hell.

Hell is the epitome of subconsciousness, and
therefore of the True Will or Hidden Sun, the sun
behind the sun symbolised by the Star of Set, Sothis.
(see also Shaitan).

Setian : A follower, or worshiper of the god Set.

Shaitan : The god of the Yezidi, who personified the
star Sothis or Sobdet. The rising of this star
heralded the inundation of the river Nile which
brought blessed relief to a sun-stricken land.

Shaman : An early priest who would adopt the guise
of an animal by wearing its skin, horns and tail. The

carrying of totem animals, later developed into the standards bearing the emblems of the popular deities of the regions, or nomes.

Shu : God of sunlight and air. Shu takes a human form wearing a plume (which is also the hieroglyphics for his name) on his head, and with his arms raised supporting the sky-goddess Nut, whom he holds apart from her consort the earth god, Geb.

Siriun : or Siriun healing, was an early type of treatment, later called hekau of healing.

Sirius : The Dog-Star. In the arcane tradition, the vast star Sirius is the sun behind the sun, the true father of our Universe. Sirius was the primordial star of all time. He was known in Egypt as the Doubling One, hence a Creator or Reflector of the Image.

Sistrum : Was the sacred instrument par excellence.

The sistrum was very much used in the services of the temple. It was made from either copper or bronze. The handle is cylindrical and is surmounted by a 'u' form, with four fine metal 'asp' shaped rods, each one holding approximately seven small metal cymbals that tinkle like tiny bells when the sistrum is shaken.

Sothis : (see Sirius)

Supreme Logos : That which 'is'; the Evolutionary Personality.

Sut : Means 'The Opener' – and Horus who 'Shuts' or 'Closes' Sut as the brother of the Sun, Horus.

Sutekh : Another name for Set.

Sut-Har : The child described from very earliest times as of dual type, so that he became known as Sut-Har or Sut-Horus. Later, the idea of twins arose, and became the Gods of the Two Horizons.

Sut-Horus : (see Sut-Har)

Sut-Typhon : The taunt flung at the Sut-Typhonians

by the Osirians, was 'Orphan', intending to brand

them as Fatherless in a religious sense because

they worshipped only the Mother and Child, who

became looked upon as the Harlot and the Bastard.

The irony is that it was accepted that the mother of

The Christ-child experienced an immaculate

Conception.

Tefnut : Primeval goddess personifying moisture. She

is the female partner of Shu.

Two Horizons : (see Sut-Har)

Udimu : A king of the First Dynasty. He is always

depicted wearing the white crown 'Hedjet', and

dressed in a closely fitted garment. This apparel

was to be copied later, when depicting the god

Osiris. The reign of Udimu pre-dates the intro-

duction of the Osirian mythology and religion, as
this king's sacred animals were the baboon i.e.
Thoth or Djehuti in conjunction with the Apis.

Universal Logos : The Great Universal Personality.
That which 'is'.

Ur-Hekau : 'The Mighty One of Spells'. The Great
Magick Power represented the thigh or khepsh of
the Goddess Nut, in which the star dwells. The term
ur-hekau connects this light with hekt, or heket, the
lunar ophidian (serpent) current represented by the
frog, lizard, hare, ape, hyena and other lunar
symbols of change, or magickal transformation.
The ancient Egyptians used a magick wand which
they called Ur-Hekau. It was in the form of a ram-
headed snake. This was the symbol of the 'Living
Word' that had its origins in feminine nature. The
ram was a symbol of Amen, and also the Age of

Aries, the Hidden God carried over from the

previous æon when the crocodile was the zoötype

of Set, the god born of the thigh of Typhon.

The custodian of this magickal wand would

be the Sem priest.

Ursa Major : Is the constellation of the Thigh which

typified the birthplace of Light in the Dark of the

Abyss. The Goddess of the seven stars of Ursa Major,

with Set the Dog-star as the annual proclaimer of

the Goddess, were reflected terrestrially as the

sixteen sanctuaries of Osiris – eight in Upper Egypt,

and eight in Lower Egypt. Nut was typified

celestially by this constellation. The seven stars of

this complex symbolised Night or Typhon and her

offspring, to which at a later time was added her

first male child, Set or Sothis. It is interesting to note

that the adze is shaped in the form of Ursa Major.

Uazet : Another form of the cobra goddess.

Uwas sceptre : A sceptre made in the likeness of the god Set. This emblem of dignity was carried by the Pharaoh during ceremonial and state occasions, regardless of whether the king was a follower of this deity.

Wadjet : Was the cobra goddess of Buto and the guardian and preserver of royal authority over Lower Egypt.

Wahab : Were the lowest rank of priests in the temple. Nevertheless, they were necessary for the daily working of the temple. All of the priesthood were very conscious about their diet, and in general, the priests abstained from most sorts of pulse, mutton and swine's flesh; and in their more solemn purification's, even excluded salt from their meals. They were as strict about their ablutions as in their diet. They bathed twice a day, and twice during the night, and some were so strict, they would only wash themselves with the water which had been tasted by the ibis.

Every third day they would shave their head and entire body. They spared no pains when it came to the promotion of cleanliness.

Grand ceremonies of purification took place in preparation to their fasts, many of which lasted from seven to forty-two days. Some would even fast for an even longer period. During this time they abstained entirely from meat, herbs and vegetables.

All other extra indulgences were put aside.

However, the priests enjoyed great privileges.

They paid no taxes, no part of their income was used for the necessary expenses of life, any land they owned was free from all duties and a state allowance of corn was given to them as well as

provision from the public stores.

Wepwawet : 'Opener-of-ways' appears originally to

have been a war god who led the king to battle, but

in later times he became a god of the dead, and was

eventually assimilated to Anubis. He is depicted as

a wolf standing on a nome standard. He is also the

original and chief deity of Abdjw, a realm later to

be usurped by Osiris

BIBLIOGRAPHY

Achad, Frater *The Egyptian Revival,* Samuel Weiser Inc., New York, 1973

Armour, Robert A. *Gods and Myths of Ancient Egypt* American University in Cairo Press, 1986

Baines J and Malek J *Atlas of Ancient Egypt*, Phaidon Press, Oxford 1996

Brunton, Dr Paul *A Search in Secret Egypt* Samuel Weiser, Inc York Beach, Maine, 1988

Budge, E A Wallis *The Book of Opening the Mouth*, Paul Kegan, Trench, Trubner, London 1909

Budge, E. A. Wallis *Gods of the Egyptians* (*Studies in Egyptian Mythology*) Dover Publications, Inc.London, 1969

Draco, Mélusine, Liber Aegyptius, Ignotus Press 1998

Grant, Kenneth *Cults of the Shadow,* Skoob Publishing, London 1994

Gurdjieff, G I *Meetings with Remarkable Men* Arkana, London 1985

Hart, George A. *Dictionary of Egyptian Gods and Goddesses,*

Routledge, London 1986

Hichens Robert *Spell of Egypt* The Century Co New York 1911

Hope, Murry *Practical Egyptian Magic*, St Martins Press, New York, USA 1986

Hornung, Erik *Conceptions of God in Ancient Egypt: The One and the Many*. Cornell University Press, New York, USA 1971

Issue 2, July-August 2000, *Cult and Funerary Temples*. Kemet Magazine

Issue 3, September-October 2000, *The Temple of Horus at Edfu*. Kemet Magazine

Issue 4, November-December 2000, *Myth and Ritual in the Temple of Horus at Edfu*. Kemet Magazine

Lawlor, Robert *Sacred Geometry*, Thames & Hudson, United Kingdom 1982:

Morenz, Siegfried. *Egyptian Religion* Cornell University Press New York, USA1973

Murray, Margaret *The Splendour that was Egypt (The Bundle of Life from Ancient Egypt)*, Sidgwick & Jackson Ltd 1972

Page, Judith *The Song of Set* Aeon, Publishing, London, 2000

Page, Judith *The Song of Meri Khem,* Mandrake of Oxford 2007

Page, Judith *The Song of Bast,* London 2010

Poe, Michael *Ancient Egyptian Metaphysics,* (personal paper)

Redford, Donald B. The *Ancient Gods Speak: A Guide to Egyptian Religion,* Oxford University Press 2002

Rice, Michael, Egypt's Making: *The Origins of Ancient Egypt 5000-2000 BC,* Routledge, Independence, Kentucky, U.S.A., 2003

Richardson, Alan and Walker-John, Billie *The Inner Guide to Egypt,* Arcania Press Bath UK 1991

Shaw, Ian and Nicholson, Paul, *The British Museum Dictionary of Ancient Egypt,* The British Museum, London 2002

St George, Elizabeth *Journey to the Cat Star,* Spook Publication, London 1990

Vernus, Pascal *The Gods of Ancient Egypt,* George Braziller, Pennsylvania, USA 1998

Watterson Barbara '*The House of Horus at Edfu. Ritual in an Ancient Egyptian Temple*' Stroud, Tempus Publishing Ltd., 1998

Wilkinson, Richard H. The *Complete Gods and Goddesses of Ancient Egypt*, Thames & Hudson, LTD London 2003

Wilkinson, Toby, *Early Dynastic Egypt*, Routledge, London 2001,

TO WRITE TO THE AUTHOR

If you would like to write to the author or would like more information about this book please write via her web site on: www.judith-page.com

Some useful websites

Paul F Newman is no ordinary Astrologer – he reads the stars. For more information: pneuma@live.co.uk

Starfire Publishing

Since 1986, when we published the first issue of Starfire, a Journal of the New Aeon, we have specialised in publishing titles that bear on Thelema. We focus in particular upon the Draconian or Typhonian tradition which is best represented today by the works of Kenneth Grant, but which may also be glimpsed in the works of others such as Aleister Crowley, Austin Osman Spare, Sir John Woodroffe, and Gerald Massey. There are also many groups and individuals that are tapping this dynamic and creative current, and in the process contributing to its present resurgence:

http://www.starfirepublishing.co.uk

Pentacle Magazine UK's premier independent Pagan magazine. Marion Pearce: http://pentaclemagazine.co.uk

Ombos House of Life is maintained by Kemetic author Mogg Morgan, on behalf of the Companions of Seth. www.ombos.co.uk

Printed in Great Britain
by Amazon.co.uk, Ltd.,
Marston Gate.